LEOPARD GECKO C

The Ultimate Guide to learn everything about how to care, feed, diet, habitat, health, breeding and tips to raising leopard geckos as pets

Jerry Milner

Table of contents

CHAPTER ONE 4

    Introduction to Leopard Geckos 4

    Amazing things to know about leopard geckos 7

CHAPTER TWO 11

    Distinctive physical characteristics 11

CHAPTER THREE 15

    Housing requirements 15

    Temperature and humidity control 19

CHAPTER FOUR 24

    Diet and Feeding 24

    Nutritional needs for your pet 28

CHAPTER FIVE 33

    Handling and socialization 33

    Proper ways to handle a Leopard Gecko 37

    Understanding Leopard Gecko Behavior 42

    Reproduction and mating rituals 47

CHAPTER SIX 52

    Common Health Concerns and Maintenance 52

    Identifying and treating prevalent health conditions
   57

    Regular maintenance and hygiene practices 63

CHAPTER SEVEN 68

Interacting with Leopard Geckos 68

Bonding with your Leopard Gecko 72

Legal restrictions and responsible ownership 76

Final thoughts on Leopard Geckos care 81

CHAPTER ONE

Introduction to Leopard Geckos

Leopard Geckos (Eublepharis macularius) belong to the reptile family Eublepharidae and are small to medium-sized. They are indigenous to the arid regions of South Asia, particularly Afghanistan, Pakistan, and sections of India, and have acquired immense popularity as pets due to their distinct appearance, manageable size, and low maintenance requirements.

The epidermis of these geckos has a mottled or blotched appearance, which gives them their distinctively stunning patterns and hues. Their skin hue can range from bright yellows and oranges to darker browns and blacks. Leopard Geckos are distinguished by their distinctive, fat-tailed appearance, which stores energy reserves and aids in balance.

Leopard Geckos are nocturnal or crepuscular by nature, meaning they are most active between dusk and dawn. They have specialized adaptations, such as vertical pupils, that enable them to efficiently navigate in low-light environments.

Leopard Geckos, unlike some other gecko species, are incapable of climbing smooth vertical surfaces due to their lack of adhesive toe pads. However, their remarkable ability to regenerate their tails makes up for it. If a Leopard Gecko loses its tail as a result of self-defense or an accident, it can regrow a new one, albeit with a slightly different appearance.

As companions, Leopard Geckos are typically docile and manageable, making them appropriate for enthusiasts of all skill levels. When adequately tended for, some individuals can live for at least 20 years.

Due to their intriguing behaviors, such as their distinct communication via tail swaying and body postures, Leopard Geckos have become popular subjects of study and observation. In addition, they engage in intricate courtship rituals during the reproductive season.

In general, Leopard Geckos are captivating creatures that offer a riveting view into the world of reptiles, making them a treasured addition to many homes.

Amazing things to know about leopard geckos

Leopard Geckos are intriguing and captivating companions for a number of reasons:

1. Leopard Geckos are visually striking due to their vibrant colors, intricate patterns, and distinctive fat-tailed appearance. Each gecko has its own distinct combination of characteristics, making them an attractive addition to the collection of any reptile enthusiast.

2. In comparison to many other species of reptiles, Leopard Geckos are relatively small and compact, attaining an average length of 8 to 10 inches. Their manageable stature makes them

simpler to care for and handle, especially for individuals with limited space or who prefer a companion that does not require a large enclosure.

3. The docile temperament of leopard geckos makes them appropriate companions for both novice and experienced reptile caretakers. They are typically accustomed to being handled and can form a bond with their caretakers, allowing for pleasurable interactions and a sense of companionship.

4. In comparison to other reptiles, Leopard Geckos have relatively simple maintenance requirements. They do not require complex illumination setups or high humidity levels, which simplifies their enclosure setup. In addition, the

majority of their diet consists of invertebrates that are commercially available, such as crickets and mealworms.

5. When properly cared for, Leopard Geckos have a relatively extended life expectancy, often reaching 15 to 20 years or more. This longevity enables pet owners to establish a long-lasting bond with their creature, as they can appreciate their companionship for an extended period of time.

6. The behavior of leopard geckos is so captivating that it captivates their caretakers. Observing and comprehending their behavior, from their nocturnal activity patterns and unique foraging strategies to their communication through tail swaying

and body language, can be a fascinating and rewarding experience.

7. The keeping of Leopard Geckos as pets provides the opportunity to learn about reptiles, their habitats, and their behaviors. Children and adults alike can cultivate an appreciation for the natural world and gain valuable insights into responsible pet ownership and conservation efforts through exposure to nature.

Overall, the combination of their alluring appearance, manageable size, docile nature, and intriguing behavior makes Leopard Geckos a desirable option for reptile enthusiasts and pet owners seeking a fascinating and engaging companion.

CHAPTER TWO

Distinctive physical characteristics

Leopard Geckos have numerous physical characteristics that contribute to their distinct appearance. These characteristics consist of:

1. Skin Patterns: The skin patterns of leopard geckos are one of their most distinctive characteristics. They have a mottled or blotched appearance, with a variety of color and pattern variations. On their bodies and tails, these patterns can include contrasting patches, stripes, or bands. Patterns can differ widely between individuals, giving each gecko a distinct appearance.

2. Leopard Geckos are distinguished by their wide, leathery tails. The function of the tail includes adipose storage, balance, and even defense. Typically, the base of the tail is broader than the tip. Leopard Geckos are capable of voluntarily shedding their tails (known as autotomy) in response to a threat or peril. The severed tail can regenerate over time, although the regenerated tail might not be identical to the original.

3. Eyes are yet another distinguishing feature of Leopard Geckos. They have large, round, distinct irises with vertical pupils. The vertical pupil aids their perception of depth and movement, enhancing their ability to hunt in low-light environments. Their irises appear

in a variety of hues, including yellow, orange, and occasionally red.

4. Leopard Geckos have epidermis that is typically smooth and faintly velvety to the touch. They lack adhesive toe pads, unlike some other reptiles, which limits their ability to scale flat vertical surfaces. Instead, they use their powerful limbs and talons to climb and move.

5. On the sides of their skulls, Leopard Geckos have well-defined, minuscule ear apertures. The epidermis covering these apertures is thin and translucent. Not only are their ears necessary for hearing, but they also detect vibrations and air pressure changes in their environment.

6. Leopard Geckos have a relatively robust and compact body structure. They are not as slender as other species of gecko. Their body is sustained by short, robust appendages with talons for mounting and grasping.

The combination of these distinctive physical characteristics contributes to Leopard Geckos' overall aesthetic appeal. Their distinctive patterns, tail structure, eye form, and other characteristics distinguish them from other reptiles and contribute to their allure as companions.

CHAPTER THREE

Housing requirements

Leopard Geckos require a suitable habitat to maintain their health and wellbeing. Here are the most important accommodation considerations:

1. Leopard Geckos necessitate a capacious habitat to facilitate their activity and thermoregulation. The minimum recommended aquarium size for a single adult gecko is 20 gallons, but enclosures of 30 to 40 gallons are preferable. Allowing for natural behaviors and promoting overall contentment by providing ample space.

2. Choose a substrate that is both cleanable and secure. Options include reptile carpet, paper towels, slate tiles, and shelf liner without adhesive. When

feeding, avoid loose substrates such as sand or wood fragments, as they pose a risk of ingestion and impaction if inadvertently consumed.

3. Provide numerous concealing places within the enclosure so Leopard Geckos can feel secure and exhibit their natural behavior. Create concealment spots at both the warm and cold extremities of the enclosure with reptile skins, caverns, or cork bark.

4. Establish a suitable temperature gradient within the terrarium to facilitate thermoregulation. Place a heat mat or heat cloth on one side of the tank to produce a toasty area between 88 and 92 degrees Fahrenheit (31 and 33 degrees Celsius). The opposite side should be colder, with temperatures

between 75 and 80 degrees Fahrenheit (24 and 27 degrees Celsius). Utilize a thermostat to regulate and prevent excess of the heat source.

5. Leopard Geckos are predominantly nocturnal and therefore do not require UVB illumination. However, supplying a low-wattage incandescent or LED light with a day/night cycle can help maintain a consistent routine and improve the gecko's visibility. Provide a concealment site where the gecko can escape the light if it so chooses.

6. Leopard geckos are native to desolate regions and therefore require a low humidity level. Target a relative humidity range of 30-40%. The enclosure does not require regular sprinkling, but a moist hide, such as a

small box filled with moistened vegetation, can be provided to assist in shedding.

7. Environmental Enrichment: Enhance the gecko's habitat with the proper ornamentation and environmental enrichment. This may include branches, pebbles, artificial plants, and a modest basin of water for imbibing and bathing.

8. Regularly sanitize the enclosure by removing trash and spot-cleaning contaminated spots. Monthly, perform a comprehensive cleansing of the entire enclosure, including replacement of the substrate. This helps maintain a clear and sanitary habitat for your gecko.

To establish a suitable and comfortable habitat for Leopard Geckos, it is essential to research and comprehend their specific habitation requirements. Providing optimal housing conditions improves their physical and mental health, allowing them to flourish in captivity.

Temperature and humidity control

Temperature and humidity regulation are essential for sustaining optimal conditions within the enclosure of a leopard gecko. Here are the most important temperature and humidity considerations:

Temperature:

1. Create a heated basking area on one side of the enclosure, with temperatures between 88 and 92 degrees Fahrenheit (31 and 33 degrees

Celsius). This creates a thermally optimal environment for digestion, metabolism, and general health.

2. The opposing side of the enclosure should be colder, with temperatures between 75 and 80 degrees Fahrenheit (24 and 27 degrees Celsius). This enables the gecko to modulate its body temperature and find solace when necessary.

3. Heating Equipment: Use a heating pad or heat mat designated for reptiles under the tank. Place it under one side of the tank so that it covers approximately one-third of the floor area of the enclosure. Connect the heating pad to a thermostat for temperature regulation and maintenance. This prevents the gecko

from overheating and guarantees its safety.

4. Monitor the temperature on both the heated and cold surfaces of the enclosure using a dependable digital thermometer or temperature pistol. Regularly inspect and, if necessary, modify the heating apparatus to maintain the desired temperature gradient.

Humidity:

1. Leopard Geckos are native to arid regions and require moderately low levels of humidity. Target a relative humidity range of 30-40%. Excessive humidity can cause respiratory problems and skin issues in geckos.

2. Use a digital hygrometer to monitor the relative humidity levels within the

enclosure. To obtain an accurate reading of the overall humidity, position the hygrometer centrally.

3. Providing an arid environment is the typical method for controlling humidity in the enclosure of a leopard gecko. Avoid sprinkling or spraying the enclosure excessively. However, ensure the enclosure contains a humid hide to assist in shedding. As a humid conceal, a small receptacle loaded with moist vegetation or eco-earth can be utilized.

4. During shedding, marginally increasing the humidity by sprinkling the humid hide or providing a moistened area can aid the gecko in shedding. To avoid complications, remove any slough that remains on the gecko's body.

Remember to monitor and modify the temperature and humidity levels on a regular basis, particularly during different seasons or when the room's environment changes. Providing your Leopard Gecko with proper temperature and humidity control ensures a comfortable and healthy habitat.

CHAPTER FOUR

Diet and Feeding

Diet and dietary habits are essential aspects of Leopard Geckos' maintenance. Here are some guidelines to consider:

1. Leopard Geckos are insectivores, which means that the majority of their diet consists of insects. As their primary dietary source, provide a variety of appropriately sized invertebrates. Insects such as crickets, mealworms, dubia roaches, and waxworms are commonly consumed. Before feeding insects to a gecko, they are stuffed with nutritive food, which increases their nutritional value.

2. Prey measure: The measure of the prey should be proportional to the

gecko's size. To prevent suffocation hazards, insects should typically be no larger than the breadth of the gecko's cranium. As the gecko develops, the prey should be adjusted proportionately.

3. The metabolic rate of juvenile Leopard Geckos is higher than that of adults, so they should be fed more frequently. Feed gecko juveniles daily or every other day. Geckos can be fed every two to three days as adults. However, monitor the gecko's weight and, if necessary, modify its nutrition schedule to maintain a healthy body condition.

4. Calcium and Vitamin Supplementation: Provide calcium and vitamin supplements to ensure

appropriate nutrition. Before feeding the insects to the gecko, dust them with a calcium supplement powder. Once or twice per month, take a vitamin supplement to prevent deficiencies.

5. Always offer a modest dish of clean, fresh water in the enclosure. Each day, the water must be replaced to maintain its purity. Leopard Geckos will imbibe as required from the water receptacle. In addition, some geckos may enjoy the intermittent sprinkling of water particles on their epidermis for hydration purposes.

6. Time of Feeding and Observation: Leopard Geckos are crepuscular, which means they are most active at dawn and twilight. Provide sustenance at

these periods to correspond with their natural feeding habits. Observe the dietary habits and appetite of the gecko. A robust gecko will actively pursue its prey and ingest it.

7. Some geckos may have trouble capturing fast-moving insects, or they may not be as aggressive consumers. In such cases, you can attempt hand-feeding or feeding the gecko with feeding utensils. This ensures that they receive adequate nutrition.

8. It is crucial not to overfeed Leopard Geckos, as gluttony can result in health issues. Depending on the gecko's size and age, provide an adequate number of insects at each feeding session. Adjust portion sizes as necessary to maintain a healthful weight.

Observing your gecko's feeding habits, tail girth, and general body condition can help you determine if their diet is adequate and if adjustments are required. Providing your Leopard Gecko with a balanced and varied diet will contribute to its health and well-being.

Nutritional needs for your pet

To maintain their overall health and well-being, leopard geckos have particular nutritional requirements. Here are the primary dietary concerns for Leopard Geckos:

1. Protein: Leopard Geckos must consume an abundance of high-quality animal protein in their diet. Protein-rich insects consisting of crickets, mealworms, dubia roaches, and waxworms. Offer live invertebrates of

the appropriate size to accommodate the gecko's size and age.

2. It is essential to provide a varied diet to ensure a balanced nutrient intake. Alternate between insect species to provide a diversity of nutrients and prevent nutritional deficiency. This mimics the gecko's grazing behavior in the environment.

3. Calcium is required for appropriate bone growth and maintenance in Leopard Geckos. Calcium supplements are essential for preventing metabolic bone disease. Before feeding the insects to the gecko, dust them with a calcium supplement powder. In addition, provide a calcium supplement for the gecko to ingest as necessary.

4. Vitamin D3 is required for optimal calcium absorption and utilization. It is necessary to prevent calcium deficiency. Some calcium supplements already contain vitamin D3, but if not, provide a once- or twice-monthly vitamin D3 supplement. Geckos that are exposed to UVB radiation can also produce vitamin D3 naturally.

5. Gut-loading refers to the practice of feeding nutritious foods to insects prior to offering them to a gecko. This increases the nutritional value of the invertebrates, providing the gecko with a more nutritious meal. Before feeding, provide the insects with gut-loading foods such as leafy greens, carrots, and sweet potatoes or commercial gut-loading diets for at least 24 to 48 hours.

6. Although Leopard Geckos obtain the majority of their water from their prey, it is essential to provide a modest basin of clean, fresh water in the enclosure. Each day, the water must be replaced to ensure its purity and sustenance.

7. Monitoring and Adjustments: Monitor the gecko's body condition and weight on a regular basis. Adjust the quantity and frequency of feedings in order to maintain a healthy weight and prevent obesity or malnutrition.

It is essential to remember that the nutritional requirements of Leopard Geckos can vary depending on their age, size, reproductive status, and overall health. Consultation with a reptile veterinarian or experienced reptile caretaker can provide valuable guidance for customizing your gecko's diet to suit its specific nutritional requirements. For the long-term health and vitality of your Leopard Gecko, it is essential to provide a balanced and nutrient-dense diet.

CHAPTER FIVE

Handling and socialization

Manipulation and socialization can be beneficial for Leopard Geckos, but it is essential to approach these activities with caution and consideration for the gecko's natural behaviors and preferences. Here are some handling and socialization tips for leopard geckos:

1. Before attempting to handle a new Leopard Gecko, it is essential to allow it time to acclimate to its new environment after bringing it home. Provide them with a stable and stress-free environment for at least a week or two without disturbing their enclosure.

2. After the gecko has had time to acclimate, introduce delicate, brief

handling sessions. Calmly approach the gecko and avoid abrupt movements that could startle or stress it. Handle with unhurried and deliberate motions.

3. Hand Position: When lifting up a Leopard Gecko, support their weight by placing your hand underneath their torso. This can cause discomfort or harm to the gecko. Be mindful of their fragile appendages and refrain from yanking or twisting on them.

4. Keep handling sessions comparatively brief, particularly at the outset. Start with a few minutes and progressively increase the duration as the gecko grows more accustomed to its surroundings. Consider any indications of tension or distress, such as growling, tail twitching, or

attempting to flee. If the gecko exhibits symptoms of tension, restore it gingerly to its enclosure.

5. Positive Reinforcement: During management sessions, use positive reinforcement. After successful handling, provide modest treats or incentives so the animal will associate the experience with something positive. This can assist the gecko in forming a favorable association with handling and social interaction.

6. Aim for routine but infrequent handling sessions, particularly with adult geckos. Generally, once or twice per week is sufficient. Avoid handling the gecko excessively or unnecessarily, as it can cause tension and disrupt its natural routine.

7. Respect Individual Preferences: It is essential to acknowledge that not all Leopard Geckos appreciate or tolerate handling to the same degree. Some geckos may be more accustomed to being handled, whereas others may prefer to be left alone. Consider the inclinations of your gecko and modify your interactions accordingly.

8. Always supervise handling sessions, particularly when minors are present. Leopard Geckos can be fragile, and accidents are possible. Provide a calm and controlled environment to reduce potential hazards.

Keep in mind that each gecko is unique, and their tolerance for handling can vary. Observe their body language and reaction to handling cues. If a gecko consistently exhibits signs of tension or distress during handling, it may be best to minimize or eliminate handling and instead concentrate on providing a stimulating and enriching environment within its enclosure.

Building a positive and trustworthy relationship with your Leopard Gecko requires time and effort. Respect their boundaries and provide socialization opportunities that correspond with their specific requirements and preferences.

Proper ways to handle a Leopard Gecko

To ensure the comfort and safety of a Leopard Gecko, handling it requires a delicate and cautious approach. Here are some correct techniques for handling a Leopard Gecko:

1. Be sure to thoroughly cleanse your hands with detergent and water before handling a Leopard Gecko. This eliminates any contaminants or aromas on your hands that could potentially stress or damage the gecko.

2. Approach Slowly and Calmly: To avoid alarming or straining the gecko, approach it slowly and calmly. Geckos can become agitated or defensive in response to sudden movements and startling sounds.

3. When lifting up a Leopard Gecko, place one hand under the animal's body to support its weight. Ensure you are not gripping or grasping the object too securely by applying a light and moderate amount of pressure. In your

hand, the gecko should feel secure and at ease.

4. Avoid Grasping the Tail: The tail of a Leopard Gecko is delicate and easily wounded by inappropriate handling. Avoid grasping or dragging the gecko by the tail, as doing so can cause tension, injury, or even loss of the tail.

5. Keep Sessions Brief: Especially at first, keep handling sessions brief so the gecko can acclimate and adapt to being handled. Beginning with a few minutes, progressively increase the duration as the gecko becomes acclimated to being handled.

6. Observe Signs of Stress: During handling, pay close attention to the gecko's body language and behavior. Indicators of tension include growling,

twitching the tail, attempting to flee, and attacking. If any of these symptoms are present, return the gecko to its enclosure and attempt again later.

7. Handle on a Low Surface: Leopard Geckos should be handled on a low surface, such as a table or the floor. This decreases the possibility of accidental accidents or injuries from a greater height.

8. Although socializing with your Leopard Gecko is beneficial, it is essential to avoid handling it excessively. Leopard Geckos are reclusive by nature and do not need constant interaction. Allow the gecko ample time to unwind and investigate its enclosure without interruption.

9. Leopard Geckos are ectothermic, which means that their body temperature is regulated by the environment. Before handling the gecko, ensure that your hands are at an appropriate temperature to prevent temperature shock. Before handling, warm your hands by pressing them together or using a hand warmer if they are chilly.

Remember that each Leopard Gecko is an individual with varying levels of familiarity with handling. Respect their limits and observe their reaction to handling indications. If the gecko consistently displays signs of tension or discomfort, it may be best to limit handling and instead concentrate on providing a comfortable and stimulating environment in which they can flourish.

Understanding Leopard Gecko Behavior

Understanding the behavior of Leopard Geckos will allow you to provide them with the proper care and a positive environment. Key aspects of Leopard Gecko behavior include:

1. Leopard Geckos are predominantly nocturnal, meaning that they are most active at night. They have adapted to low-light environments and have superior night vision. During their active hours, it is essential to provide them with a dim and calm environment.

2. Leopard Geckos are reclusive reptiles by nature. They typically reside alone and have their own territories in the outdoors. In the presence of other

geckos, they may become agitated or anxious.

3. Leopard Geckos are natural burrowers and prefer concealing in concealed locations. Furnish their enclosure with multiple concealment spots, such as caverns, hollow timbers, and commercial hides. These concealing places make them feel secure and protected.

4. The tail of a Leopard Gecko functions as a fat reserve and plays an essential role in the animal's overall health. As a defense mechanism, Leopard Geckos may lose their tails in times of tension or danger. This is referred to as "tail autotomy." The tail will regenerate over time, but it may have a distinct aspect.

5. Leopard Geckos are not noted for their vocalizations. They communicate primarily through body language, such as waving their tails or posturing. Hissing or vocalizations are uncommon and typically a sign of extreme tension or discomfort.

6. Leopard Geckos frequently exhibit the behavior of twitching their tails. In response to prospective threats, territorial disputes, or during courtship displays, they may twitch their tails. Consider the gecko's overall body language in order to comprehend the context of the tail fluttering behavior.

7. Leopard Geckos have scent receptors on the undersides of their legs for scent marking. By pressing against objects in their enclosure, they

may use these organs to designate their territory. This behavior aids in establishing their presence and deters would-be intruders.

8. Temperature Regulation Leopard Geckos are ectothermic, meaning they regulate their body temperature using external heat sources. To maintain their preferred body temperature, they will move between warmer and colder locations within their enclosure.

9. Exploration and hunting Leopard geckos are naturally inquisitive and appreciate investigating their environment. Within their enclosure, they may climb on branches, boulders, and other structures. Additionally, they possess natural foraging instincts and

will actively pursue and capture living prey.

10. Leopard Geckos possess an acute sensitivity to vibrations. They are able to detect movement and vibrations in their environment, allowing them to locate prey and avoid potential threats.

Observing and comprehending the behavior of your Leopard Gecko will allow you to identify their requirements and provide the appropriate care. It is essential to create a stress-free and stimulating environment that allows captive animals to exhibit their natural behaviors and flourish.

Reproduction and mating rituals

Reproduction and mating rituals are intriguing aspects of the behavior of leopard gecko. Here is a summary of the reproduction of Leopard Geckos:

1. Male and female Leopard Geckos exhibit sexual dimorphism, which means there are visible distinctions between the sexes. Males tend to be slightly larger than females, and their undersides feature a prominent V-shaped series of pre-anal apertures. In addition, males have hemipenal bulges at the tail's base.

2. Sexual Maturity: Leopard Geckos reach sexual maturity between 8 and 12 months of age, but this varies. It is crucial not to propagate geckos too young, as this can endanger their health.

3. Breeding Season Leopard Geckos breed seasonally, and their reproductive activity is affected by variations in temperature and daylight. Breeders frequently simulate the natural reproductive season in captivity by manipulating illumination and temperature conditions.

4. Male Leopard Geckos engage in courtship rituals in order to allure females. Typical ritual behaviors include head swaying, tail flapping, and circling. Males may also communicate with females through whistling or clicking noises.

5. Once courtship has been effective, copulation occurs. The male approaches the female from behind and transfers sperm into her cloaca using

his hemipenes. The duration of copulation can range from minutes to hours.

6. Egg Development and Laying: Following a successful mating, the female Leopard Gecko will produce eggs internally. The period of development, known as gestation, lasts approximately 20 to 30 days. After excavating a nesting site in the substrate, females will deposit their eggs there. Typically, a clutch contains between one and three eggs, though larger clutches are possible.

7. Incubation of Leopard Gecko embryos requires specific environmental conditions. The optimal temperature range for incubation is 82 to 86 degrees Fahrenheit (28 to 30

degrees Celsius). Typically, the incubation period lasts between 45 and 60 days, depending on the incubation temperature.

8. Once the period of incubation has concluded, the eggs will hatch, and tiny hatchlings will emerge. The hatchlings of the leopard gecko are self-sufficient and do not require parental care. It is essential to provide the hatchlings with suitable accommodations and care to ensure their survival.

Breeding Leopard Geckos should be conducted responsibly and with a comprehensive comprehension of their care needs. Temperature, illumination, and nutrition are essential for successful reproduction and the health of the geckos involved. If you are considering breeding Leopard Geckos, you should conduct research and consult with experienced breeders or herpetologists to ensure that the process is conducted ethically and in the geckos' best interest.

CHAPTER SIX

Common Health Concerns and Maintenance

Leopard Geckos are typically robust reptiles, but they can encounter health problems. Regular maintenance and monitoring are essential for their health. Here are some prevalent Leopard Gecko health concerns and care practices:

1. Leopard Geckos periodically discard their epidermis to facilitate development. Furnish a moist hide in their enclosure to facilitate in the process of molting. If a gecko has difficulty shedding, it may need assistance removing any debris that has become trapped on its body.

2. Leopard Geckos can be affected by parasites, including mange and intestinal worms. Regularly observe your gecko for signs of parasites, such as weight loss, appetite changes, and aberrant excrement. If you suspect that your reptile has a parasite infestation, you should consult a reptile veterinarian for diagnosis and treatment.

3. Impaction occurs when a gecko consumes indigestible substrate or extraneous objects, resulting in a blockage in the digestive tract. Use a substrate that reduces the risk of impaction, such as paper towels or reptile carpet, particularly for geckos that are prone to ingesting substrate, such as juveniles.

4. MBD is a common condition caused by a calcium and vitamin D3 deficiency or an improper calcium-to-phosphorus ratio in the diet. It can cause brittle bones, deformities, and other severe health issues. Provide a calcium-rich diet, UVB illumination, and calcium supplements as directed by your veterinarian for your gecko.

5. Infections of the Respiratory Tract Leopard geckos are susceptible to respiratory infections due to inadequate temperatures, humidity, or poor husbandry practices. A respiratory infection is characterized by wheezing, open-mouth respiration, excessive mucous, and appetite loss. If you suspect your pet has a respiratory infection, seek immediate veterinary care.

6. Mouth Rot: Mouth rot, also known as infectious stomatitis, is a mouth infection characterized by inflamed or distended gums, excessive saliva, and difficulty swallowing. Mouth decay can be caused by improper oral hygiene, trauma, or bacterial/fungal infections. Dental hygiene and a tidy environment can help prevent this condition.

7. It is recommended to schedule routine checkups with a reptile veterinarian in order to monitor your gecko's health, determine their weight, and resolve any concerns.
Veterinarians with expertise in reptile care are able to offer advice on appropriate husbandry practices and diagnose and treat any health problems that may develop.

8. Maintain a clean and sanitary environment for your Leopard Gecko. Remove feces, uneaten food, and shed skin from the enclosure on a regular basis. Periodically clean and disinfect the enclosure, but avoid caustic chemicals that may be toxic to geckos. Ensure that pure water is available daily.

9. Temperature and Humidity Monitoring: Maintain the enclosure's optimal temperature and humidity levels. Use a dependable thermometer and hygrometer to regularly monitor these parameters. Incorrect temperature and humidity can cause health problems, such as respiratory issues and difficulty flaking.

10. Balanced Diet: Offer your Leopard Gecko a balanced and nutritious diet. Feed them appropriately sized invertebrates sprinkled with calcium powder, such as crickets or mealworms. Provide a varied diet to ensure that they receive a wide range of nutrients.

By maintaining good husbandry practices, monitoring your gecko's health, and seeking veterinary care when necessary, you can prevent and treat common health issues, thereby ensuring that your Leopard Gecko will live a long and healthy life.

Identifying and treating prevalent health conditions

It is essential to identify and treat common health problems in Leopard Geckos for their overall well-being.

While it is always recommended to consult a reptile veterinarian for a precise diagnosis and treatment plan, the following are some common health issues you may encounter with Leopard Geckos, as well as general guidelines for identifying and treating them:

1. Infestations Caused by Pests:

Weight loss, decreased appetite, aberrant feces, and visible parasites (such as mites) on the gecko's body are symptoms.

o Treatment: Consult a veterinarian specializing in reptiles for a fecal examination and anti-parasitic medication. Isolate infected geckos and sanitize their enclosures meticulously to prevent reinfestation.

2. Respiratory Illnesses:

o Symptoms include wheezing, mouth-to-nose respiration, nasal discharge, loss of appetite, and lethargy.

o Treatment: Seek immediate veterinary care. Antibiotics or other medications may be prescribed by the veterinarian to treat the infection. Ensure the enclosure's temperature and humidity levels are optimal for recovery.

3. MBD: Metabolic Bone Disease

o Manifestations: Weakness, tremors, distended joints, deformities, bone softening or bending.

o Treatment: Consult a veterinarian specializing in reptiles for a comprehensive evaluation and treatment plan. Correcting calcium and vitamin D3 deficiencies, modifying the diet, and providing adequate UVB illumination may be part of the treatment. In severe cases, more intensive care may be required.

4. Oral Fungus (Infectious Stomatitis):

o Symptoms: distended or inflamed gums, excessive saliva, reluctance to consume, lesions or mucus in the mouth.

o Treatment: Seek immediate veterinary care. Typically, treatment consists of cleansing the mouth, administering appropriate antibiotics or antifungal medication, and addressing any underlying causes, such as poor oral hygiene or trauma.

5. Impaction:

o Symptoms: loss of appetite, constipation, bloating, lack of bowel movements, and lethargy.

o Treatment: Immediately consult a reptile veterinarian if you suspect impaction. In severe cases, the veterinarian may recommend dietary changes, hydration methods, or manual removal of the obstruction.

6. Infected or Wounded Skin:

o Symptoms include redness, inflammation, ulcers, scabs, aberrant discharge, and excessive clawing.

o Treatment: Maintain a sanitary enclosure and provide suitable concealment places. Consult a reptile veterinarian for diagnosis and treatment, which may involve topical medications or antibiotics, if you observe any lesions or skin abnormalities.

7. Eye Problems:

o Symptoms include swollen or contracted eyes, discharge, cloudiness, and trouble opening the eyes.

o Treatment: Seek immediate veterinary care. Eye problems may require specialized treatment, such as eye medications or ointments, if they are severe.

For appropriate diagnosis and treatment of any health issues in Leopard Geckos, it is essential to consult a reptile veterinarian. They can provide customized recommendations based on the specific requirements of your gecko and help ensure the highest quality of care.

Regular maintenance and hygiene practices

Regular maintenance and hygiene practices are essential for keeping your Leopard Gecko's habitat clean and healthy. Here are some essential practices to observe:

1. Exterior Cleaning:

o Remove waste: Remove excrement and uneaten food from the enclosure on a regular basis. Daily spot cleaning will prevent the accumulation of refuse.

If using a loose substrate, such as sand or coconut fiber, the contaminated substrate must be replaced frequently. This may involve partial or comprehensive substrate alterations, depending on the substrate variety.

o Disinfection: Periodically disinfect the enclosure to prevent detrimental bacteria or parasite growth. Use disinfectants that are safe for reptiles and follow the instructions provided. Before you reintroduce your gecko, thoroughly rinse to eradicate any residue.

2. Water Management:

o Clean water dish Every day, remove any debris or refuse from the water dish. Replace the water with dechlorinated, purified water.

3. Controlling Humidity and Moisture:

o Maintain proper humidity levels: Monitor and maintain proper humidity levels in accordance with Leopard Geckos' particular needs. Typically, this falls between 30 and 40 percent.

o Prevent excess moisture: Prevent excessive moisture accumulation in the enclosure, as it can promote bacterial or fungal growth. Ensure adequate ventilation and substrate selections that permit moisture evaporation.

4. Hiding Places and Design:

o Clean and inspect concealing places: Routinely clean and inspect hiding places, such as caverns or logs, to remove any refuse or detritus that has accumulated. This helps keep your gecko's concealment spot tidy and secure.

o Clean and disinfect all decorative objects, such as branches and pebbles, on a periodic basis to eliminate potential sources of pathogens or parasites.

5. Handling and Personal Hygiene:

Before and after handling your Leopard Gecko, thoroughly cleanse your hands with detergent and tepid water. This aids in preventing the spread of bacteria and other potential pathogens.

o Avoid cross-contamination: If you have multiple reptiles, use distinct handling tools, cleaning supplies, and enclosures for each individual.

6. Routine Health Examinations:

o Monitor the health of your gecko: Observe your gecko frequently for any changes in behavior, appetite, or physical appearance. Respond immediately to any concerns or anomalies.

o Schedule veterinary examinations: Schedule regular examinations with a reptile veterinarian to ensure your gecko's overall health and to receive expert advice on proper care and maintenance.

By adhering to these regular maintenance and hygiene practices, you can help create a clean and healthy living environment for your Leopard Gecko, thereby reducing the risk of health problems and promoting their health.

CHAPTER SEVEN

Interacting with Leopard Geckos

The experience of interacting with Leopard Geckos can be rewarding. Even though they may not be as social or interactive as other companions, they are still capable of displaying curiosity and acclimating to human presence. Here are some tips on how to interact with Leopard Geckos:

1. Respect their behavior: Leopard Geckos are typically docile and placid, but they may feel threatened or agitated by harsh handling or excessive movement. Respect their boundaries and observe their body language. If they exhibit signs of tension, such as a quivering tail, snarling, or attempting to flee, it is best to give them space.

2. Before handling your gecko, thoroughly cleanse your hands with detergent and tepid water. This assists in removing any strong odors or residues that may aggravate or stress your gecko.

3. Utilize a gradual and delicate approach when lifting up your gecko. Do not grasp or squeeze them. Use both hands to lift them up from underneath, supporting their body and allowing them to feel safe.

4. Keep handling sessions brief, especially in the beginning, so that your gecko can become accustomed to your contact. Start with a few minutes and progressively increase the duration as your gecko grows accustomed to its surroundings.

5. Before handling, ensure that the immediate environment is secure and escape-proof. Close all doors, windows, and other apertures to prevent the gecko from becoming lost or injured by accident.

6. Although occasional handling is acceptable, Leopard Geckos are predominantly reclusive creatures that prefer their own territory. Avoid excessive handling and frequent disruptions, as they can cause tension and negatively affect their health.

7. Hand-feeding: Hand-feeding can be a trust-building and bonding activity. Allow the gecko to approach and consume the sustenance (such as mealworms or insects) at its own leisure.

8. Allow your gecko to investigate and interact outside of its enclosure in a safe and controlled environment. Prepare a secure and supervised space, such as a reptile playpen or a designated area devoid of potential dangers.

9. Observe and appreciate: Spend time observing the natural behaviors and routines of your gecko. They can be intriguing to observe, and through observation, you can learn more about their unique characteristics and preferences.

Remember that each gecko has its own personality and level of comfort around humans. Some geckos may be more tolerant of human interaction than others. Always prioritize the health and happiness of your gecko, and adapt your interactions accordingly. Establishing a bond and gaining trust requires time and patient, so allow your gecko to dictate the interaction's pacing.

Bonding with your Leopard Gecko

Bonding with your Leopard Gecko is a gradual process involving establishing trust and associating your presence with positive experiences. Leopard Geckos may not demonstrate affection in the same manner as mammals, but they can adapt to human interaction and recognize their caregivers. Here are some relationship guidelines for your Leopard Gecko:

1. Respect their space and behavior: Permit your gecko to acclimate to its new environment and feel safe in its

enclosure. Avoid sudden movements, harsh sounds, and handling that may cause your gecko stress or alarm. When they exhibit signs of tension or distress, observe their behavior and body language and give them space.

2. Spend time in the vicinity of your gecko's enclosure on a regular basis. This enables them to associate your presence with positive events, such as feeding and cleansing.

3. Hand-feeding your gecko can help establish trust and associate your presence with positive reinforcements. Allow the gecko to approach and consume the sustenance (such as mealworms or insects) at its own leisure.

4. Slow and delicate handling: Introduce handling sessions gradually, beginning with brief durations and gradually increasing them over time. When lifting up your gecko, use gradual and delicate motions to support their body and make them feel safe. Avoid handling that is abrupt or forceful, as it may cause tension.

5. Taming sessions: Schedule taming sessions in which you interact with your gecko outside of its enclosure in a tranquil and controlled environment. Utilize a reptile playpen or an area devoid of potential hazards. Permit your gecko to investigate and interact at its own pace, rewarding it with treats or a target stick.

6. Leopard Geckos have an acute sense of smell, allowing them to bond through olfactory communication. You can transmit your fragrance by wiping your hands on clean, non-toxic items placed in the enclosure, such as a boulder or hide. This can help acclimate your gecko to your fragrance over time.

7. While handling or interacting with your gecko, use a quiet, reassuring voice and delicate contact. Avoid sudden movements and harsh sounds that could frighten or upset them. If they appear comfortable, stroke their back or head with a light contact.

8. Building trust and a relationship with your gecko requires perseverance and consistency. Each gecko is distinctive,

and the procedure may vary. Respect the gecko's boundaries and comfort level, and be consistent in your interactions with it.

Keep in mind that not all geckos are equally receptive to bonding, as their personalities vary. Some geckos may be more reticent and less receptive to direct interaction. Respect their preferences and avoid forcing interaction if they exhibit signs of tension or discomfort. Focus on establishing a trusting relationship with your gecko, and take pleasure in observing their natural behaviors and distinctive characteristics.

Legal restrictions and responsible ownership

Legal restrictions and responsible ownership play a crucial role in assuring the health and conservation of Leopard Geckos and their natural populations. It is essential to comprehend and abide by any legal requirements and guidelines associated with the ownership and care of Leopard Geckos. Here are some important considerations:

1. Before procuring a Leopard Gecko, familiarize yourself with the local laws and regulations pertaining to pet ownership, particularly reptiles. Certain jurisdictions may require specific permits, licenses, or restrictions on the ownership of Leopard Geckos and other reptiles. Ensure that you adhere to these regulations to avoid legal trouble.

2. Purchase Leopard Geckos from breeders or pet stores that prioritize

the health, well-being, and responsible propagation of their reptiles. Avoid supporting illegal wildlife traffic and purchasing geckos from unreliable sources.

3. Before bringing a Leopard Gecko into your home, familiarize yourself with its specific maintenance requirements. Research their dietary demands, lodging requirements, temperature and humidity preferences, and other aspects of their care that are essential. Provide a physical and behavioral environment that is suitable and stimulating.

4. Leopard Geckos have an average duration of 10 to 20 years, so you should be prepared for a long-term commitment. Consider your ability to

provide appropriate care, sufficient time for interaction and maintenance, and financial resources for their ongoing requirements, including veterinary care.

5. Veterinarian care: Provide your Leopard Gecko with routine veterinary examinations to ensure their health and well-being. Find a veterinarian with experience with reptiles who can provide appropriate medical care, preventative remedies, and dietary and husbandry advice.

6. If you intend to propagate Leopard Geckos, you should be aware of the responsibilities and considerations associated with responsible reproduction. Ensure that you have the required knowledge, resources, and

permits (if applicable) to engage in responsible reproduction practices.

7. To prevent the discharge of non-native species, captive Leopard Geckos should never be released into the wild. The introduction of non-native species can harm local ecosystems and native fauna populations. If you can no longer care for your gecko, seek out responsible options such as finding a reputable new proprietor, surrendering to a rescue organization, or contacting adoption agencies that specialize in reptiles.

8. Continuous education and learning: Keep abreast of the most recent developments in Leopard Gecko care, husbandry methods, and conservation efforts. Educate yourself on best

practices on a regular basis to ensure the optimal care and health of your gecko.

By adhering to legal restrictions, being a responsible owner, and providing proper care, you as a responsible reptile enthusiast contribute to the well-being of Leopard Geckos and support their conservation.

Final thoughts on Leopard Geckos care

Leopard Geckos inhabit a world that is truly captivating due to its unique characteristics and attractiveness. Due to their unique physical characteristics and docile nature, as well as their enthralling behaviors and low maintenance care needs, they have become popular companions among reptile enthusiasts. Their beautiful patterns and hues, combined with their adaptability to a variety of habitats, make them a visually arresting and fascinating species to observe and care for.

While ownership of a Leopard Gecko requires responsibility and dedication, forming a connection with these reptiles can be extremely rewarding. Through patient handling, respectful interaction, and appropriate care, you can earn the trust of these captivating creatures and appreciate their company.

Remember that Leopard Geckos flourish in environments that imitate their natural habitat by providing them with suitable temperatures, humidity, and concealing places. By creating a safe and stimulating environment, you can promote their natural behaviors and ensure their well-being.

In addition, responsible ownership necessitates awareness of legal requirements, support for reputable breeders, and consideration of conservation efforts to protect Leopard Geckos and their natural counterparts.

Whether you are a seasoned reptile devotee or just commencing your voyage into the world of Leopard Geckos, these distinctive creatures offer an opportunity to develop a deeper appreciation for the beauty and diversity of the animal domain.

Printed in Great Britain
by Amazon